Hello, everybody!

My name's Margarita. I'm the princess, the girl who Diego Velázquez painted in his picture *The Family of Phillip IV*, which is also called *Las Meninas* or *The Maids of Honour*, in 1656, when I was five years old.

I've been here, in the Prado Museum, for a long, long time, for nearly two centuries, since it was opened in 1819. That's why I can tell you that I've seen all the important things that have happened in this big building.

The Museum is in an avenue called the Paseo del Prado, in Madrid. It's one of the most important in the world and thousands of people from countries all around the world come and visit us.

It deserves to be famous because of the variety and reputation of the paintings, sculptures, drawings, furniture and other works of art on show here.

The Prado Museum is considered Spain's greatest art gallery. It's one of the world's most important museums of paintings and there are now almost 8,000 pictures in its collection.

If you want, I can tell you the story of the Museum.

Are you ready? Then let's go!

The Museum's beginnings

I'm going to explain to you some of the unusual things about this Museum, which is now my home. Well, first of all I must tell you that in the beginning it wasn't as big, and it didn't have as many works of art.

This story starts at the end of the eighteenth century with an idea. A court painter, a German called Anton Raphael Mengs, suggested to King Charles III that it would be a good idea to gather together and out on show to the public all the works of art that the different Kings of Spain had obtained for their private collections. But that king, Charles III, who did so many other things for Madrid and the Kingdom of Spain, didn't take Meng's advice during his reign.

The years passed, and in the middle of the War of Independence, in 1809, Joseph Bonaparte, brother of the famous Napoleon, arrived in Spain. He was named King and forced on the Spanish people, and decided to build a Josephine Museum modelled on the Louvre Museum in Paris. But Joseph didn't have much luck in his attempt, either, as it remained just a project that was never carried out.

But the idea of a Museum to bring together all those royal collections persisted. During the reign of Ferdinand VII, Charles III's grandson, the Royal Academy of Fine Arts asked him about the idea several times, and he agreed to it, and his second wife, María Isabel de Braganza, was also interested and supported the project. So Ferdinand VII made it possible for Madrid to have an important museum at last, which was called the Royal Museum of Painting and Sculpture.

The Museum opened on 19 November 1819. But unfortunately, Queen María Isabel, who had had so much to do with the project, was not able to attend, as she had died in 1818.

As a sign of gratitude of the Queen's support in the founding of the museum, the artist José Álvarez de Pereira was commissioned to produce a sculpture of her, with the Queen sitting down, as if she was welcoming visitors to the Museum. In 1829, the painter Bernardo López Piquer painted a full portrait of the same Queen, with her left hand on some plans, and her right hand pointing to a window through which you can see the Museum building in the background. Both works are on display in the building.

The Museum buildings

The building chosen as the Museum's home was part of the city planning project started by King Charles III, who was known as Madrid's best mayor because of his interest in making Spain's capital beautiful and improving it. He wanted Madrid to have buildings and monuments like the ones in other big European cities.

Charles III's city planning project went from what is today the Plaza de Cibeles to the Glorieta de Atocha, making a nice wide avenue, the Salón del Prado. It was given this name, *Prado*, because José de Hermosilla's project was centred on what was then the meadow (or Prado in Spanish) called San Jerónimo del Real. This was an area with a lot of vegetation and trees, and at that time was a place for the people of Madrid to meet and relax. Several monumental fountains were built along this avenue. They were designed by the architect Ventura Rodríguez and dedicated to gods of classical mythology —Cibeles, Apollo and Neptune. Over the years, this avenue became known as the Paseo del Prado, and the name of the Museum comes from that. As you can see, you can go for an interesting walk around the Museum and visit these beautiful paintings. I'm sure you'll like them.

Along the avenue, King Charles III ordered buildings to be constructed. These would be used for science, and Juan de Villanueva was made the architect responsible for this project.

One of these buildings would house the Natural Sciences Museum, another, the Botanical Garden/Museum, would be used for observing Nature, and the third, the Astronomical Observatory, would be for looking at the sky.

The Natural Sciences Museum project was approved by King Charles III in 1785, and work on it started immediately. But the building was never finished. During the War of Independence (1808-1813), the part that had been built was used as a cavalry barracks and a gunpowder store by Napoleon's armies during their time in Madrid. So, after the war, the looting of building materials and ten years exposed to the elements, the half-finished building was in a sorry state.

1808-1813

After the war was over, King Ferdinand VII decided to create a museum using the artistic collections that belonged to the Spanish crown. With his advisers, he studied different buildings that could have been used, and decided to restore and finish the beautiful neo-Classical building that had been started over thirty years previously.

He placed Antonio López Aguado in charge of carrying out the necessary work, and he used Juan de Villanueva's original plans and scale model. This scale model can be seen in the Museum today. It is made from pine and boxwood and is nearly four metres long.

The King paid for all the remodelling and fitting out of the building as a museum out of his own pocket. At the end of 1819 the Royal Museum of Painting and Sculpture was opened. This took up only the north wing of the building, as work still had not finished. Moreover, the decoration of the outside of the building was slow and painstaking, and the main facade was not finished until 1850.

The building is in three parts, joined by two galleries. The parts at the sides are two cubes, while the central one is shaped like a basilica with a gateway decorated with six columns. Above it is a large frieze showing Ferdinand VII as the Protector of the Sciences, Art and technology. Behind the figure of the King are the mythological gods Minerva, Apollo, Mercury and Neptune, and a lion is lying at his feet. This main facade, looking onto the Paseo del Prado Avenue, has a double decoration in the two sections of the building's central gallery. There are twelve feminine sculptures of a symbolic nature inside the niches and sixteen medallions with busts of the most outstanding Spanish artists - painters, sculptors and architects – on both sides of the gate leading to the Paseo del Prado, which is also called the West Gate or Velázquez's Gate. This is because in front of it there is a sculpture of the painter, with which Spanish artists commemorated the third centenary of his birth in 1899.

In the northern part of the building, opposite a statue of the painter Francisco de Goya, there are now two doors. One of these leads to the building's ground floor, and the other to the first floor at the end of a long staircase decorated with columns.

The first floor of the south facade is decorated with columns and on the ground floor is the South Gate, also called Murillo's Gate. And opposite is the entrance to the Botanical Gardens with a small square with a statue of that painter in the centre.

The combination of granite, the pink colour of the bricks and the harmony of its architecture, as well as the decoration of the outside, make the building particularly beautiful, and it is now considered a Spanish national monument and a symbol of culture.

When it was included in the Prado Museum, the nineteenth and early twentieth century collections were moved there. In 1981, this building received what was known as Picasso's Legacy, and with it, one of the artist's most famous works, *Guernica*, which was later moved to the Museo Nacional Centro de Arte Reina Sofía, very near the Paseo del Prado, where important twentieth century paintings are exhibited.

Extension, maintenance, conservation and fitting work has not stopped since the Museum was opened and continues today. As you can see, the Museum has grown throughout its history, and is still growing in the present.

Extensions to the museum

After it opened, and as the years went by, the Museum became too small to put all its works of art on show. For this reason, it was necessary to carry out the first extension (1914-1921), which extended the building at the back, including a line of showrooms with open-air courtyards.

The next renovation was carried out in the 1950s, and this added another line of showrooms to those built in the previous extension. In the 1960s, the open courtyards were closed off to make them into showrooms, storage and toilets.

Despite all this work, as time passed there was more and more need for space to show off the important collections properly. As a solution, in 1971 the Casón del Buen Retiro, which is in the nearby Felipe IV Street, became part of the Museum. This building was designed by the architect Alonso Carbonell and was the dance hall of the Palacio del Buen Retiro, the palace for rest and relaxation that King Phillip IV ordered to be built. The ceiling of the dance hall, which was painted by the Italian painter Lucas Jordán at the end of the seventeenth century, is still preserved today. After being abandoned — which is how it got its name Casón, meaning large old house— was extended in the nineteenth century, and the two main facades, acing Felipe IV Street and Alfonso XII Street, were built in the neo-classical style.

The Prado Museum in the nineteenth Century

The first works of art to arrive at the Museum in 1818 were the paintings that had come from the Palacio Real, the Palacio de Aranjuez, the Palacio de La Granja, and other royal palaces. So at that time it had over 1,600 paintings. Despite this, when the Museum was opened only three and eleven paintings, by the painters Velázquez, Murillo, Ribera, Zurbarán, Goya —who was still alive— and other great Spanish masters went on display in the northern part of the building.

Those in charge of the Museum selected some forty works by Diego Velázquez. Among these was my painting, *Las Meninas*, which was moved from the Palacio Real in Madrid to the museum. So I've been living here in the Museum since 1819.

The *Gaceta de Madrid* —which was the leading newspaper of the time— gave the news of the museum's opening the day before, and talked about King Ferdinand VII's interest in his subjects' welfare and in spreading the Fine Arts and in raising his people's awareness of them. The *Gaceta* also told its readers that starting from the next day, the 19th of November, the Museum would be open for eight days running, except for when it rained and when the streets were muddy. For the rest of the year, from then on, it would open its doors every Wednesday, from nine o'clock in the morning until two in the afternoon, although visitors needed special permission from the Royal Court.

As Ferdinand VII was really the owner of all the works of art on display and in storage in the Museum —paintings, sculptures and decoration— he would pay for the maintenance himself.

Later, after the 1868 revolution and the expulsion of Isabel II, the Museum was given to the people and its collection became the property of the State. Its name was also changed, to the *Museo Nacional del Prado*, or National Museum of the Prado. In 1873, the government of the First Spanish Republic decided to add to the Museum's artistic property by including more than two thousand works of art. These came from another museum open at the time in the Trinidad Convent, which came from convents and monasteries that had been closed by Mendizábal's Law in 1854.

The Prado Museum continued to receive more works of art belonging to the Spanish Crown and others that until that time had been kept in the San Fernando Fine Arts Academy. The Museum also stared to buy works of art to increase its collection.

In 1826, the Museum closed for two years to restore and prepare new rooms, which were used to improve the organisation of the exhibitions.

After Ferdinand VII died in 1833, the collection was inherited by his two daughters, the future Queen Isabel II and Luisa Fernanda. To avoid the collection being divided between them, the director of the Royal Museum —at that time the Duke of Híjar— suggested that Isabel buy the rights to half the collection from her sister Luisa Fernanda. The idea was accepted by the Queen Regent María Cristina and that's what happened. It was the first time in history that works of art in the Museum had been valued.

As the Museum was receiving other donations and was buying new works at that time, the difficulty of storing and exhibiting such a large amount of works forced it to start a policy of loans to government departments and other museums, which led to what was called the «dispersed Prado».

A strange chapter in the Museum's history happened in the year 1891. The newspaper *El Liberal*, in its edition of 25th November, published an article by Mariano de Cavia —one of the most important journalists of the time— with a title that drew all the readers' attention: «Last night's catastrophe. Spain in mourning. Fire in the Paintings Museum».

Fortunately, it was a false piece of news which the journalist, Mariano de Cavia, wanted to use to attract the attention of the general public and the government in particular to the Museum's lack of safety measures. For that reason, the next day he published another article: «Why Did The Paintings Museum Burn Down?» where he explained that he had invented the disaster to prevent it happening in the future. Of course, the consequences were not slow in coming. Various fire prevention measures were taken, the Museum's directors —who at that time were chosen from famous painters— were prohibited from setting up their workshops there, and living accommodation for the Museum's staff was built in two twin pavilions at the rear of the building.

The Prado Museum in the twentieth Century

In 1912, the *Real Patronato del Museo*, or Royal Museum Trust, was set up to solve its work and preservation problems, and was responsible for its day-to-day running and making its exhibitions and development into a model for other museums.

Life in the Museum was more or less calm until 1918, when the celebrations of its centenary were being prepared. A few months before, the Museum was robbed. The thieves stole part of what was called the Dauphin's treasure, a seventeenth crockery service that had belonged to the Dauphin —the heir to the French throne— and which his son, our first king of the Bourbon dynasty, Phillip V, bought to Spain. It was found, but some pieces no longer had their decorations and others had been destroyed to remove their precious stones and metals.

Another difficult time for the Museum and its collections was the Spanish Civil War of 1936-39. The Museum was closed to the public for those three years. The government of the Second Spanish Republic named Pablo Picasso as Director of the Prado, but this was just an honorary title as Francisco J. Sánchez Cantón was the real director at this time. The pictures had to be taken out of their frames and all the works protected from fires and bombing. The government of the Second Spanish Republic also named a Board in charge conserving and protecting all the State's artistic treasures and especially those in the Prado. Many works from the Palacio Real, El Escorial and other museums and churches were taken to the Villanueva building, where they were more protected from the dangers of the war.

Madrid was on the frontline and there was a serious danger from bombing. The Museum and the area around it suffered from the bombs but the works of art inside were not seriously damaged.

Because of the risks, the government decided to leave Madrid and the Museum's most important works of art —among them, my painting, *Las Meninas*— followed the government first to Valencia and later, to the north of Catalonia, to the province of Gerona. Eventually, the war got too close, and finally all the works were sent to Switzerland, at that time the safest country. Thanks to the help of the International Committee, they were safely taken to the United Nations headquarters in Geneva.

This move was only successful thanks to the help of artists and intellectuals of the time, like the poet Rafael Alberti, the writer María Teresa León, the painters Timoteo Pérez Rubio, Josep Maria Sert, Josep Renau and Ignacio Zuloaga, as well as the work of many other less well-known people.

When the war finished in 1939, some of these works of art were returned to Spain and the Museum once again opened its doors to visitors. The works that remained in Geneva —among them, my painting, *Las Meninas*— were used in the Exhibition «Masterpieces from the Prado Museum», which was held in Geneva in June, July and August of that year, and showed a selection of the Museum's best works. For the advertising poster and leaflets, the organisers chose a portrait of my mother, Mariana of Austria, painted by Velázquez. The exhibition was very successful, but it closed hurriedly at the end of August, and the works of art were sent back to Spain, at great risk, as the Second World War had started in Europe.

At last, I was back in my Prado Museum again.

In the years after the Spanish Civil War, having got its collections back, the Museum had to live through a time which was very difficult for most Spaniards. Once those years were over, it was again visited by foreign tourists who came to get to know Spain, and deservedly became one of the world's most visited museums. This made more work necessary, including air conditioning, lighting, security systems, restoration workshop extensions, and the building of a library, a conference room, rest areas for visitors, cafeterias, shops and bookshops.

In 1980, the Friends of the Prado Museum Foundation was set up, and its members helped the Museum by publishing books, guidebooks and leaflets and buying new works of art. In 1985, the Museum became a State-run Independent Institution, which allowed it to improve its day to day running and organise its resources and staff better.

The Prado Museum in the twenty-first Century

At the end of the twentieth century, the Museum's serious space and infrastructure problems meant that work on the Villanueva building and the Casón del Buen Retiro was necessary, but this has not been enough for a great museum like the Prado.

For this reason, in 1999 the Ministry of Culture announced a competition for extending and renovating the Museum, and the world's best architects took part. The jury chose a project presented by the Spanish architect Rafael Moneo. The following year, after several discussions and studies, some changes were made, and the final version of extension and renovation project for a new Prado Museum, with five buildings, was agreed upon.

Work started in 2001 and will go on until 2005. When it is finished, the main building will still be the Villanueva building, where the basic collection — paintings from the Middle Ages to Goya and classical and modern sculptures— will be. The Casón del Buen Retiro will be the home of the permanent exhibition of nineteenth century paintings and sculptures. Paintings from the seventeenth century royal palaces, including works by Velázquez, Zurbarán and Rubens, will be in the Salón de Reinos (an old building that used to be the Army Museum).

A new building based around the arches of the cloister of the Los Jerónimos Church, will be used for temporary exhibitions, with a new auditorium, stores that can be visited, restoration services, as well as spaces for the visiting public, like bookshops, restaurants and libraries. Finally, the Museum's offices and management will be in another building in Ruíz de Alarcón Street, very near the main building.

The collections

As I said at the beginning of this story, the Prado Museum has one of the most important collections of paintings, drawings and engravings, as well as classical and modern sculptures. In total, there are nearly 17,000 works of art. There also collections of coins, medals, furniture and decorations.

One of the most interesting collections is known as the *Dauphin's Treasure*, and is on show in the basement underneath the Villanueva building, and is carefully protected. It has trays, jugs, glasses, cups and other crockery, made from rock crystal and decorated with precious stones, gold and glazes. King Phillip V brought it to Spain, as I said before.

Of all the objects in this collection, I especially like the agate salt cellar, decorated with gold and precious stones, and a dolphin carrying a shell shaped like a tray, made out of rock crystal and gold-plated silver.

But more than anything else, the Prado Museum is one of the world's most important paintings galleries. It is only possible to exhibit a small selection of the works in its collection, because there are so many and so little available space. Remember, the Museum still receives new works of art, either by buying them or because of donations.

The Spanish painting collection is the most complete collection in the world. It includes works of art from the twelfth to the eighteenth centuries, and among them we can admire paintings by masters like El Greco, Ribera, Velázquez, Zurbarán, Alonso Cano, Murillo and Goya.

There are also works on display from the nineteenth and the beginning of the twentieth centuries, by painters like Vicente López, José and Federico Madrazo, Antonio Esquivel, Eduardo Rosales, Mariano Fortuny and Joaquín Sorolla.

The Flemish Collection is also very wide-ranging, with works of art by Roger Van der Wyden and El Bosco, and the Baroque painters Peter Paul Rubens and Anthony Van Dyck.

Another of the Museum's great treasures is its Italian Painting collection, made up of paintings by Fray Angélico, Botticelli, Rafael, Titian, Tintoretto and Caravaggio. The Museum's collection also includes important works from the French, German, English and Dutch schools.

ROGER VAN DE WEYDEN

As you can see, as well as the long history of the Museum and its buildings, all of its works of art have many stories behind them. If each of them told us where it came from, and told us about its painter or artist, the reasons why it was produced, the society and culture it represents, and its trials and tribulations before arriving here, we would have a never-ending story. Or if the people shown in all these paintings, drawings and sculptures told us about their lives and adventures…

Now I'll tell you my own short story. I'm the daughter of King Phillip IV and his queen, Mariana of Austria. Diego Velázquez, the great painter, painted me several times and some of my pictures have ended up in different museums, like the Louvre in Paris, the Museum of Western Art, in Kiev, and in Vienna.

But Velázquez's great painting, which immortalised me, is *The Family of Philp IV*, also known as *Las Meninas*, or *The Maids of Honour*, which is what the young ladies whose job at court was to entertain the children and keep them company were called. They appear next to me in the painting.

Velázquez painted me in the centre of the picture, with two young ladies, two maids of honour, and the jesters Maribárbola and Nicolasillo, who is playing with a mastiff dog at his feet. Behind them is an older lady and a gentleman, while in the background, through the half-open door, you can see José Nieto, a gentleman.

The painter included himself on the left of the picture, in front of a big canvas. It's one of his best self-portraits. My parents are also there, but they're reflected in a mirror at the back of the room.

In this painting, Velázquez showed a typical day in our lives at the Alcázar palace in Madrid. I liked watching Velázquez paint in his workshop very much. My painting is like a big open window on this workshop. Look carefully at the painting. Who do you think Velázquez was painting? Me, or my parents, the King and Queen? It's the painter's and the period's masterpiece. He knew how to paint light, shadow, colour and even the draughts in the room where we were at that moment.

This painting was in the Alcázar palace in Madrid, the old Royal Palace for many years. After a serious fire, it was moved to the new Palacio Real, and finally, as I said at the beginning, to the Prado Museum in 1819. Now, in the Villanueva building, we are in the best place in the most important and beautiful room in the whole museum, which is called *La Sala de Velázquez*, or «Velazquez's Room».

From my picture I receive all the visitors to the Museum and I'd like you to come and see me one day. I'll be waiting for you here. See you soon!